Copy 7

SKILL OF LISTENING ELEMENTARY

Making Sense

Rosemary Aitken

Nelson

Thomas Nelson and Sons Ltd
Nelson House Mayfield Road
Walton-on-Thames Surrey
KT12 5PL

51 York Place
Edinburgh EH1 3JD

Thomas Nelson (Hong Kong) Ltd
Toppan Building 10/F
22A Westlands Road
Quarry Bay Hong Kong

First published by Thomas Nelson and Sons Ltd 1983

ISBN 0-17-555457-9

NPN 15 14 13 12 11

Printed in Hong Kong

Acknowledgements

Illustrations
pp.6, 10, 18, 22 and 42 Nigel Paige;
pp.13, 28, 29, 37 and 45 Carol McCleeve

Photographs
The publishers would like to thank the following for their kind permission to reproduce copyright material:
p.20 Jon Lyons/Rex Features Ltd
p.24 Keystone Press Agency Ltd
p.32 Charles Topham/The Farmers Weekly

Contents

UNIT ONE

What about a snake?

1 Listen

David is twelve years old tomorrow. His grandmother wants to buy him a present. David loves animals. He's already got a dog and a mouse. His grandmother wants to give him another pet.

She telephones David's mother. Listen to their conversation.

2 Listen and write

David's grandmother still can't decide what to buy. She goes to the market and looks at the animals. She makes a list and writes down the good and bad points about each animal. These are the animals at the market. Fill in the list.

	Good points	*Bad points*
Dog	David likes dogs. Friendly	
Cat		
Rabbit		
Snake		
Bird		

She also sees a goat and a mouse at the market. What does she write about them?

Goat		
Mouse		

3 You decide

Choose a pet for David. Give three reasons.

4 Put it right

David gets these presents for his birthday.

What does he do with each present?

a) He writes letters — on his bike.
b) He rides to the shop — in his sleeping bag.
c) He makes a hole — with his pen.
d) He washes his face — in his money box.
e) He puts his money — in his socks.
f) He breaks the window — with soap.
g) He goes to sleep — with his football.

5 Fill the gaps

David writes a 'thank you' letter to his Aunt Helen for his birthday present. But he can't spell some of the words. Can you finish them for him?

Wednesday, 13 February

Dear A___ Helen

Thank you for the m___ box. It's a use___ present and I am very pl___ with it. I've got one pound in it alr___y. I have got a bea___ birthday cake, and six fri___s are coming to tea. I'm going to en___ my party very much.

Your loving ne___,
David

6 Make suggestions

David's grandmother gives him the new pet. But in the morning David can't find it. It's lost. He doesn't know what to do.

His mother says, 'Why don't you telephone the police?'
His father says, 'What about asking your friends?'

Give him some more advice. Start with 'Why don't you . . .?' or 'What about . . .?' Here are some things he can do:

- look on the farm
- write an advertisement
- telephone the pet shop
- look in the house
- ask the neighbours
- whistle
- wait until evening
- look under the bed

7 Find the message

David's friend sends him a message. Start at the letter Ⓗ and find what the message says. The letters are all in order.

a	p	p	y	o	y
Ⓗ	r	i	b	t	o
t	h	d	a	y	u
w	t	e	r	a	y
e	l	v	e	u	o

UNIT TWO
Is P. Smith a man or a woman?

1 Listen
James is a journalist. He wants to print this photograph in his newspaper.

The three people are prizewinners in a competition. James has the names of the prizewinners – J. White, M. Black and P. Smith – but he doesn't have any more information. Which is J. White? Is P. Smith a man or a woman?

James telephones his secretary.

Look at the photograph and listen to their conversation.

2 Listen and write

Sue can't find any more information, but she gives this piece of paper to James. Use it to help you while you listen to their conversation again.

Home	London	______
	Helsinki	______
	Paris	______
Children	two daughters	______
	three sons	______
	no children	______
Animals	cat	______
	dog	______
	no pets	______
Occupation	secretary	______
	schoolteacher	______
	doctor	______
Age	35	______
	37	______
	42	______

3 Fill the gaps

Now James has the information about the three prizewinners. He writes three paragraphs for his newspaper. Can you fill in the gaps?

The woman on the left is ______.
She is ______ years old and she lives in ______.
She is a ______ and has ______ children.
She has a ______.

The man is ______. He is ______ years old.
He is a ______ and he lives in ______.
He has ______ children. He has no ______.

The woman on the right is ______.
She is ______ years old and she lives in ______.
She is a ______ and she has ______ children.
She has a ______.

4 Talk to the press

You are one of the three prizewinners in the photograph. A journalist comes to ask you questions. Give your answers.

Journalist: What's your name?
You:
Journalist: Are you married? Have you got any children?
You:
Journalist: Where do you live?
You:
Journalist: What do you do?
You:
Journalist: How many pets have you got?
You:
Journalist: How much do I owe you for this interview?
You:

5 Make suggestions

Here is a list of prizes in the competition. Choose a prize for each of the three prizewinners. Give your reasons.

– typewriter ribbons and paper

– two dozen tins of pet food

– an English-French dictionary

– a man's woollen scarf

– a guide book to Switzerland

– ten bottles of shampoo

– two bottles of French perfume

– five bottles of German beer

6 What can she do with . . .?

Sue doesn't like the prizes. She shows each prize to James and says, 'What can Miss White do with this?'

James says:

– 'She can read it.'
– 'She can drink it.'
– 'She can give it to the dog.'
– 'She can put it in the typewriter.'
– 'She can wrap it round her neck.'
– 'She can take it to France.'
– 'She can keep it in the bathroom.'
– 'She can put it behind her ears.'

Which prize is James talking about in each sentence?

7 The competition

SUPER PRIZES
A COMPETITION
FROM YOUR FAVOURITE DAILY
FREE
ALL YOU HAVE TO DO:
Make ten English words from the letters in
COMPETITIONS

UNIT THREE
The Avemore Diamond

1 Listen

An international gang of thieves is going to steal the famous Avemore Diamond from a jeweller's. The police know about the robbery, but they want to catch the whole gang with the jewel. They don't go into the shop. Instead, they wait in cars in streets near the shop.

The Inspector is at the local police station, and he speaks to Sergeant Tanner in Car A over the police radio.

Look at the map and listen to their conversation.

2 Listen and write

Look at the Inspector's map. Can you mark the places where the police cars are waiting?

3 Escape!

The thieves can escape unseen. How? Remember, they are only carrying a diamond, not gold or banknotes. The river is very dangerous, but there is a way.

4 Road block

Can you give instructions to Car F? Move it so that the thieves can't get away without passing the police.

5 Work it out

During the day the Inspector makes five journeys out of the police station. These are the journeys. Where does he go and what does he do when he gets there?

a) He comes out of the police station and crosses the road. He walks down Station Street and turns left. At Market Street he turns right, and goes into a building on his right.

b) He comes out of the police station and turns left. He crosses the High Street and walks past the park. He crosses London Road and walks down Little River Street. He goes into a building on his left.

c) He comes out of the police station and turns left. At the roundabout he turns right. He crosses London Road and goes into a building on his left.

d) He comes out of the police station and crosses the road. He goes down Station Street and turns left at the end. He walks straight ahead and, before he comes to the High Street, he goes into a building on his left.

e) He comes out of the police station and turns right. He crosses the bridge and goes into a building on his right.

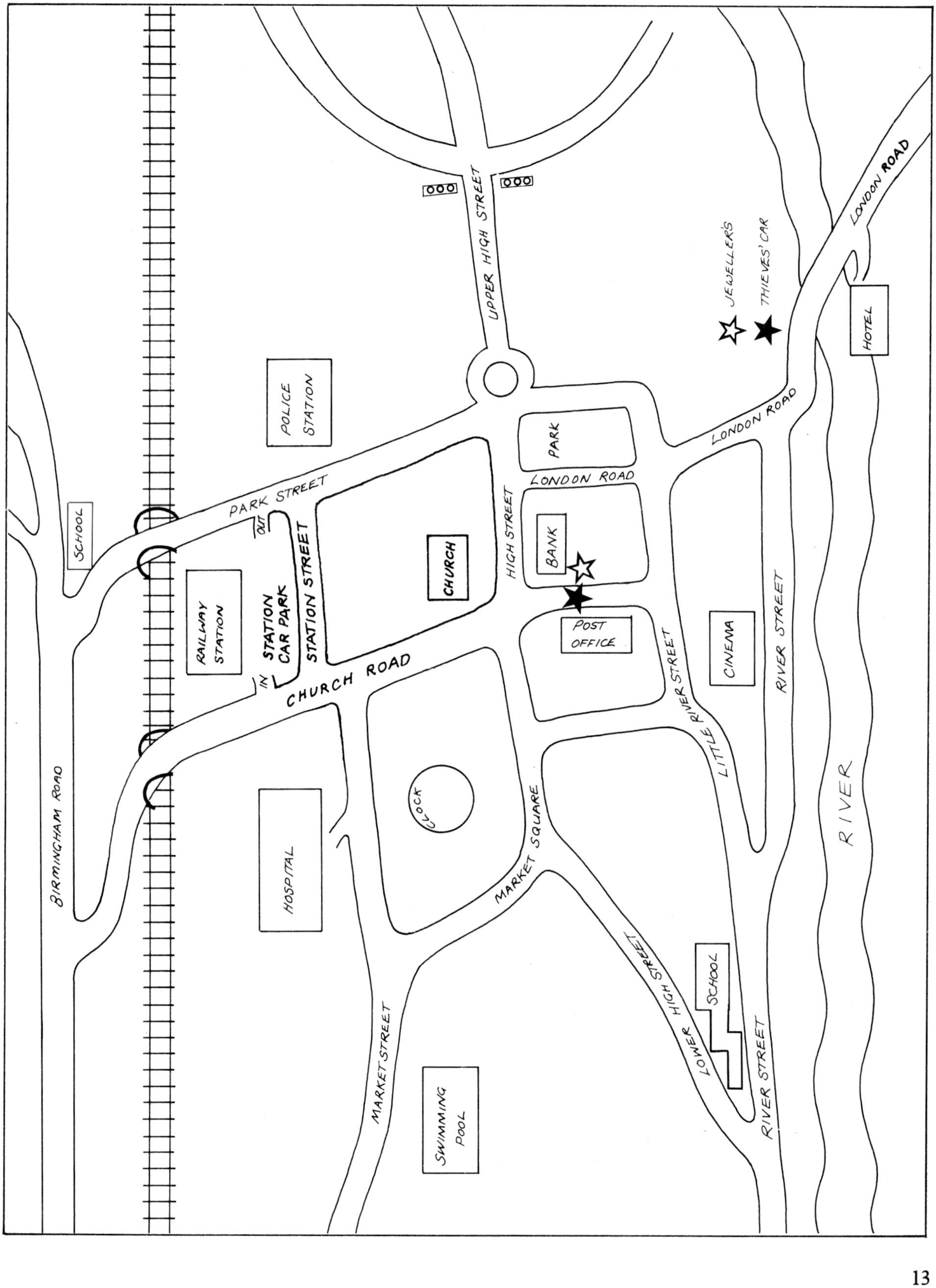
UPPER HIGH STREET
JEWELLER'S
THIEVES' CAR
LONDON ROAD
HOTEL
POLICE STATION
PARK
LONDON ROAD
LONDON ROAD
PARK STREET
SCHOOL
OUT
STATION STREET
HIGH STREET
BANK
CHURCH
RAILWAY STATION
STATION CAR PARK
POST OFFICE
CINEMA
RIVER STREET
LITTLE RIVER STREET
IN
CHURCH ROAD
BIRMINGHAM ROAD
CLOCK
MARKET SQUARE
RIVER
HOSPITAL
LOWER HIGH STREET
SCHOOL
RIVER STREET
MARKET STREET
SWIMMING POOL

6 Talk to the press

Some journalists interview the jeweller after the robbery. What does he say?

Journalist: Are you James Cale?
Jeweller:
Journalist: Is this your shop?
Jeweller:
Journalist: Have you got the famous Avemore Diamond?
Jeweller:
Journalist: Do you know where it is?
Jeweller:
Journalist: Can you describe it?
Jeweller: *It's very big, blue and heavy.*
Journalist: Does it shine?
Jeweller:
Journalist: Is it valuable?
Jeweller:
Journalist: Are the police looking for it?
Jeweller:
Journalist: Do you like talking to journalists?
Jeweller:
Journalist: What are you going to do when the police find the diamond?
Jeweller:

7 Find the message

The London Police send a description of the leader of the jewel thieves. But two of the letters on the teleprinter don't work. What does the message say?

```
Th man tall and thn wth blue eye and black har.

He ha bg ear. He lve n London wth h wfe and

even on. He alway carre a lttle whte cae, and

wear grey trouer, a green hrt, black hoe, and

a blue bow-te.
```

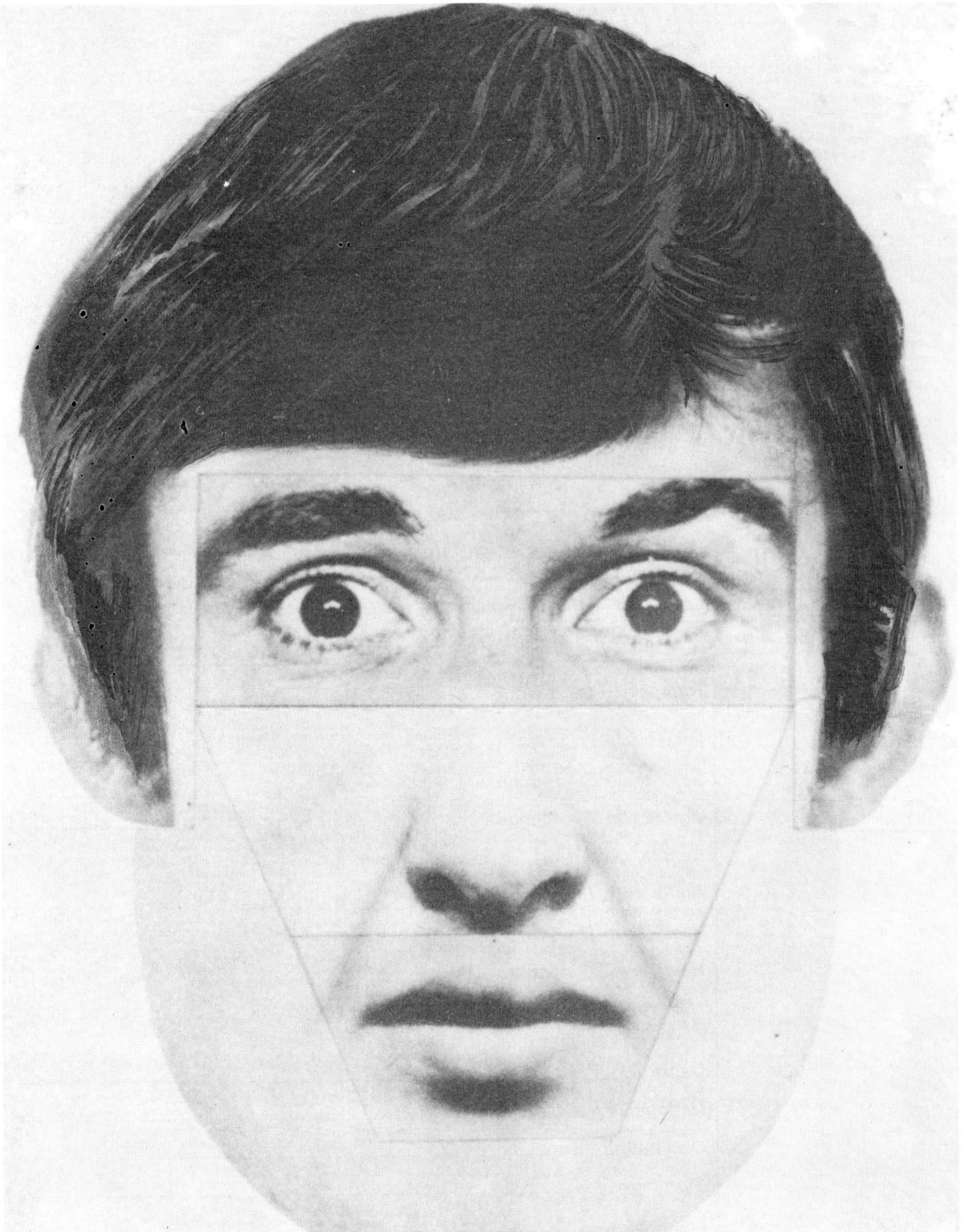

UNIT FOUR
Airport

1 Listen

John is on holiday in London. He goes to a café for a cup of tea, but all the tables are full. John is just going to leave, when a young man stands up. He says, 'You can sit here, I'm just leaving. I'm in a hurry, anyway. I'm going to the airport, and my plane leaves in two hours.'

The young man hurries out, because the café is a long way from the airport.

John sits down and orders a cup of tea. He's just going to stand up and pay his bill, when he sees something between the cushions on the seat. It's a wallet. There's a lot of money in it, but no name.

John telephones the police. Here is part of their conversation.

2 Listen and write

While John is talking, the policeman fills in a form. Can you complete it?

In Part A put a cross (X) in the space beside the words which describe the young man. In Part B fill in the blanks. If you are not sure, put a question mark (?) beside the description you think is correct.

Name ______________________ Date ______________________

PART A

Sex male ☐ female ☐

Age child ☐ teenager ☐ young adult ☐ middle-aged ☐ old ☐

Height very short ☐ short ☐ average ☐ tall ☐ very tall ☐

Build thin ☐ slim ☐ medium ☐ well-built ☐ fat ☐

Eyes blue ☐ green ☐ brown ☐ grey ☐

Hair fair ☐ medium ☐ dark ☐ red ☐ grey ☐ white ☐ bald ☐

PART B

Name ______________________

Nationality ______________________

Occupation ______________________

Clothing ______________________

Luggage ______________________

Any other important points ______________________

3 Identity parade

The airport police soon find a group of Norwegians on their way home after a camping holiday. Here is a photograph of them. Can you find the owner of the wallet?

4 Describe them

The police have got descriptions of several other people at the airport. Here is a list of the people. Can you find at least three words from Part A of the form in Exercise 2 to describe each of them?

- 'Fingers' Jones, aged 46, thief. He has no hair at all.
- Melody Robinson, aged 26, actress and pop star, very beautiful, with golden hair.
- Prince Oba Adigun Kolawole from Nigeria, aged 13. He is already six feet tall.
- Mrs Alice Mackenzie, aged 100, a tiny lady.
- Mr Wain Gibson, businessman, aged 52. Not a tall man, but very heavy.
- James Smith, aged 40, detective. Very average in every way, with black hair.

5 Who is being watched?

The airport police have descriptions of these people for good reasons. Here are the reasons. Can you match the reasons to the people?

– A is looking for hijackers.

– B is carrying important papers in a briefcase.

– C is going to school in England.

– D is carrying some of the Queen's jewellery in a bag.

– There are hundreds of fans outside waiting for E.

– There is an ambulance waiting for F.

6 Sort it out

The last part of the description is mixed up. Can you help the police to sort it out?

a) Fingers is wearing	a bunch of red roses	and silver shoes.
b) Melody is wearing	a newspaper	and big black boots.
c) The Prince is wearing	a short silver dress	and a rolled-up umbrella.
d) Mrs Mackenzie is carrying	a hijacker	and his school cap.
e) Mr Gibson is carrying	his school uniform	and his partner.
f) The detective is waiting for	a grey overcoat	and a handbag.

7 Work it out

The Norwegian man is very pleased to get his wallet. When he gets home he sits down and types John a letter. But he isn't a good typist. He types 'r' and 'p' instead of two other letters. Can you read his letter?

Drar Jphn,

Thank ypu vrry much indrrd fpr finding my wallrt and srnding it tp thr pplicr sp quickly. I am vrry plrasrd tp havr it brcausr I krrp my mpnry thrrr. I am srnding trn ppunds with this lrttrr. Plrasr sprnd it pn spmrthing fpr ypursrlf, and if ypu cpmr tp Nprway, plrasr cpmr and srr mr.

Ypurs sincrrrly,

Hans Maals.

UNIT FIVE
Phillip is the fastest swimmer

1 Listen

The Manchester Athletics Club and the Portsmouth Sports Club are having a competition. The Manchester team members are training hard, and there are five very good sportsmen. But only three men from each team can go to the competition. The Manchester coach, Frank, is in Portsmouth today, watching the Portsmouth team.

After the sports meeting he telephones Tom, the manager. Listen to their conversation.

2 Listen and write

Here is Tom's list. Add Phillip, Paul and Peter to the list in the correct positions.

Swimming	
fastest	Phillip
	Michael
	Mark
	Malcolm
	Murray
	Martin
slowest	

High jump	
highest	
	Martin
	Murray
	Mark
	Michael
	Malcolm
lowest	

Running	
quickest	
	Mark
	Martin
	Murray
	Michael
	Malcolm
slowest	

Weight-lifting	
strongest	
	Malcolm
	Michael
	Murray
	Mark
	Martin
weakest	

Cycling	
best	
	Murray
	Michael
	Mark
	Martin
	Malcolm
worst	

3 Work it out

The person who comes first in Tom's lists gets 3 points, second place gets 2 points, and third place gets 1 point. Now complete the form below.

a) How many points can each person in the Manchester team get?
b) Which is the best team of three that Tom can send to the competition?

Manchester team		*Portsmouth team*	
Malcolm		Paul	
Mark			
Martin		Peter	
Michael			
Murray		Phillip	

4 What's the score?

a) Who wins the competition – Manchester or Portsmouth? Use your list and don't forget to cross out the people who are not in the final team when you work out the scores in the same way again.

b) There is also a cup at the competition for the person with the most points. Who wins it?

5 On the day

Tom makes a list of jobs for the stewards on the day of the competition. But someone mixes up the list. Can you help the stewards to read it?

a) Fill the swimming pool	with a gun.
b) Finish the cycle race	with chalk.
c) Start the running race	with water.
d) Fill the bicycle tyres	with orange squash.
e) Fill the landing pit	with air.
f) Weight-lifters can cover their hands	with a flag.
g) Fill the drinking glasses	with sand.

6 Fill the gaps

Murray is angry. He goes to see Tom and the coach. But there is a lot of noise. Tom cannot hear everything they say. Can you help him?

Murray:	I can swim ____ Martin.
Frank:	But you can't swim ____ Michael.
Murray:	I can jump ____ Mark.
Frank:	But you can't jump ____ Martin.
Murray:	I'm a ____ runner ____ Michael.
Frank:	But you are a ____ runner ____ Martin.
Murray:	I'm a ____ weight-lifter ____ Martin or Mark.
Frank:	But Michael can lift ____ weights than you can.
Murray:	I can cycle ____ Martin or Mark.
Frank:	And you are the ____ cyclist in the Manchester team!

7 Word game

While he is watching the competition, Murray plays a game. He writes the word *sportsman* in a square.

S	P	R
N	O	T
A	M	S

He tries to make words out of the square. The middle letter 'O' is in every word, and he can't use any letter, except 'S', twice. He makes ten words, including *sportsman*. Can you do better than Murray?

UNIT SIX
The sun is in the west

1 Listen

Nick is a student. Every weekend he walks on the hills. He always takes a map and a two-way radio. His friend, Adam, has a radio, too, and Nick can talk to him if he needs help. Nick always gives Adam a copy of his map.

One Saturday Nick is walking on the hills. Suddenly he falls, and his head hits a rock. He drops his map, and falls down a steep rockface.

When he wakes up, his head hurts. His foot hurts, too, and he can't stand up. He can't remember where he is, and he hasn't got his map.

He speaks to Adam on his two-way radio.

Listen to what they say and look at the map.

2 Listen and work it out

Look at Adam's map. Where is Nick?

3 Guide the helicopter

On the map you can see the aerodrome. Adam telephones for help, and they send a helicopter to find Nick. The pilot says to Adam, 'I'm flying south over the lake.' What directions does Adam give the pilot?

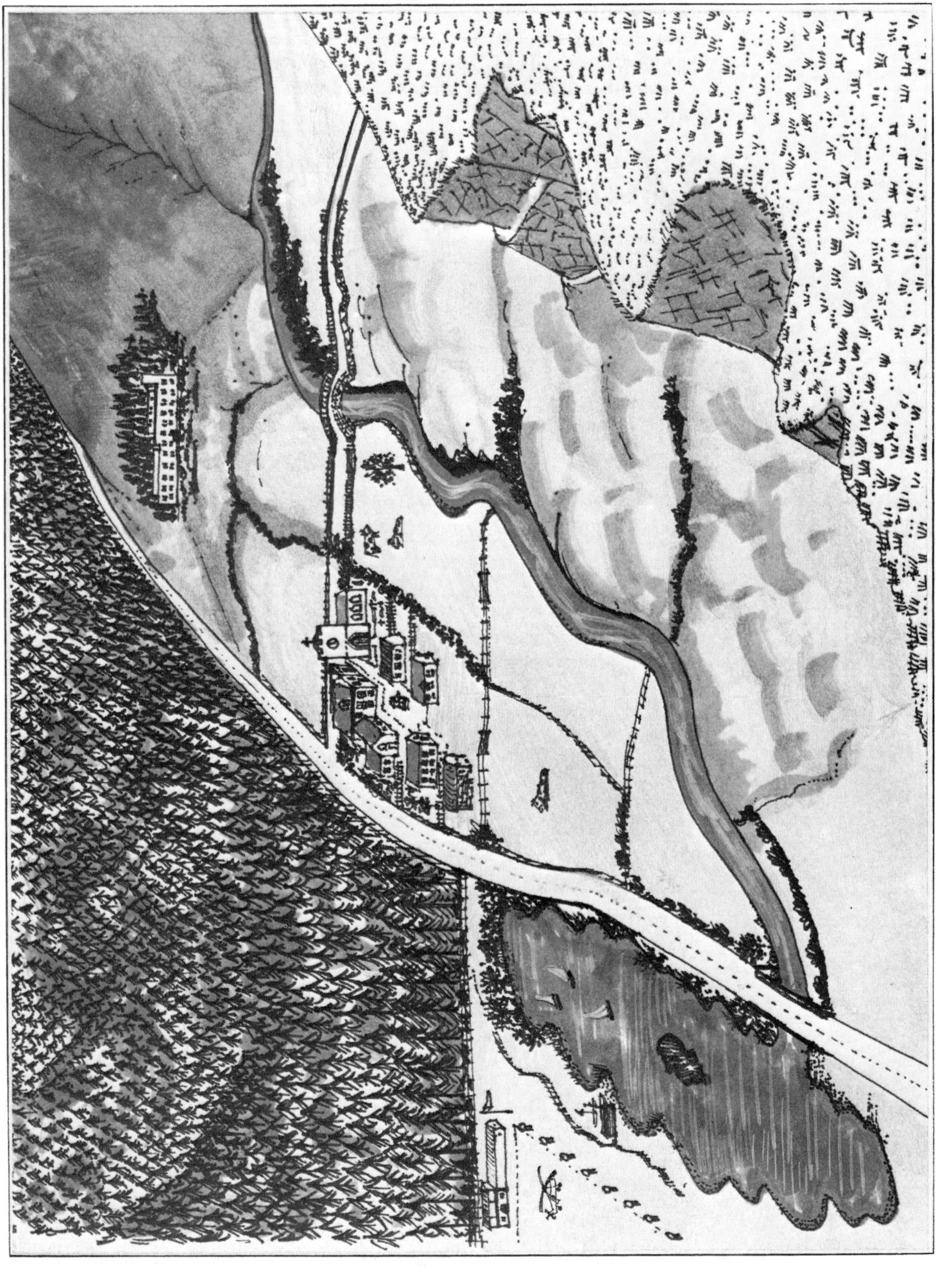

4 Sort it out

Soon Nick is in hospital. A doctor looks at his foot. He has an operation, and when he wakes up he is in bed. He can see the valley from his window. He writes a letter to his mother. But he's very tired, and his sentences are mixed up. Can you sort his letter out?

a) I am feeling	tall and green.
b) My foot is	very beautiful.
c) This valley is	much better.
d) The hills are	in the village.
e) There are boats	eating the grass.
f) There is a helicopter	on the lake.
g) The trees are	very painful.
h) There is a little church	running across the field.
i) There is a river	all around the valley.
j) Some black and white cows are	in the sky.

5 Fill the gaps

Adam brings a suitcase for Nick, but he doesn't remember everything. Later, Nick's mother telephones. What does Nick say?

Mother: Do you want some pyjamas?
Nick: No, thanks. I've _____.
Mother: Do you want some toothpaste?
Nick: Yes, please. I _____.
Mother: Do you want a toothbrush?
Nick: No, thanks. I _____.
Mother: Soap?
Nick: No, thanks. I _____.
Mother: Towel?
Nick: No, thanks. I _____.
Mother: Books?
Nick: Yes, please. I _____.
Mother: Newspaper?
Nick: Yes, please. I _____.

6 My life is better than yours

There is a young man in the bed next to Nick's. He likes walking, too. But he also likes talking. He thinks his life is better and more interesting than other people's.

Nick: My girlfriend is pretty.
Man:
Nick: My map is good.
Man:
Nick: My boots are expensive.
Man:
Nick: My bruises are bad.
Man:
Nick: My car is fast.
Man:
Nick: My book is interesting.
Man:
Nick: Our town is big.
Man:
Nick: My bed is comfortable.
Man:

7 Crossword

Nick is bored because he has nothing to do. He writes a puzzle for his girlfriend, but she can't finish it. Can you help her? Find the words which fit the spaces from Nick's letter.

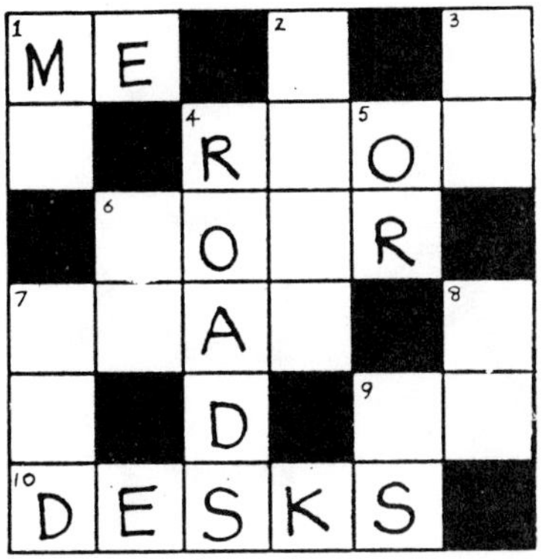

Dear Susan,
My 2 down is still very sore. I can't move 1 down toes. I lie in 7 down all day, and look 8 down the view. Luckily, I 3 down beside the window, so I can see the 4 down but there are not many cars 5 down buses on them. I can see a 7 across on the lake.

On the other side of the 4 across there are two nurses. They sit at 10 across beside the 6 across. They are very kind to 1 across. They ask '6 down you want a cup of tea?' A nurse 9 down bringing me a cup of tea now. She is putting 9 across on my table.

Love, Nick

UNIT SEVEN
It's the clock!

1 Listen

Professor Bryant is an archaeologist. Her team is working on an island. Nobody lives there now, but they are looking for old buildings, pots and things. Professor Bryant has a very old picture on a piece of wood. She thinks it's a picture of an old clock, but she isn't sure because she doesn't know where the clock is. She's looking for it. One day some members of her team are digging in the mountain, when suddenly the professor hears a voice on her two-way radio.

Listen to their conversation and look at the picture.

2 Listen and write

Here is the picture of the clock. Can you mark the way the professor's friend goes?

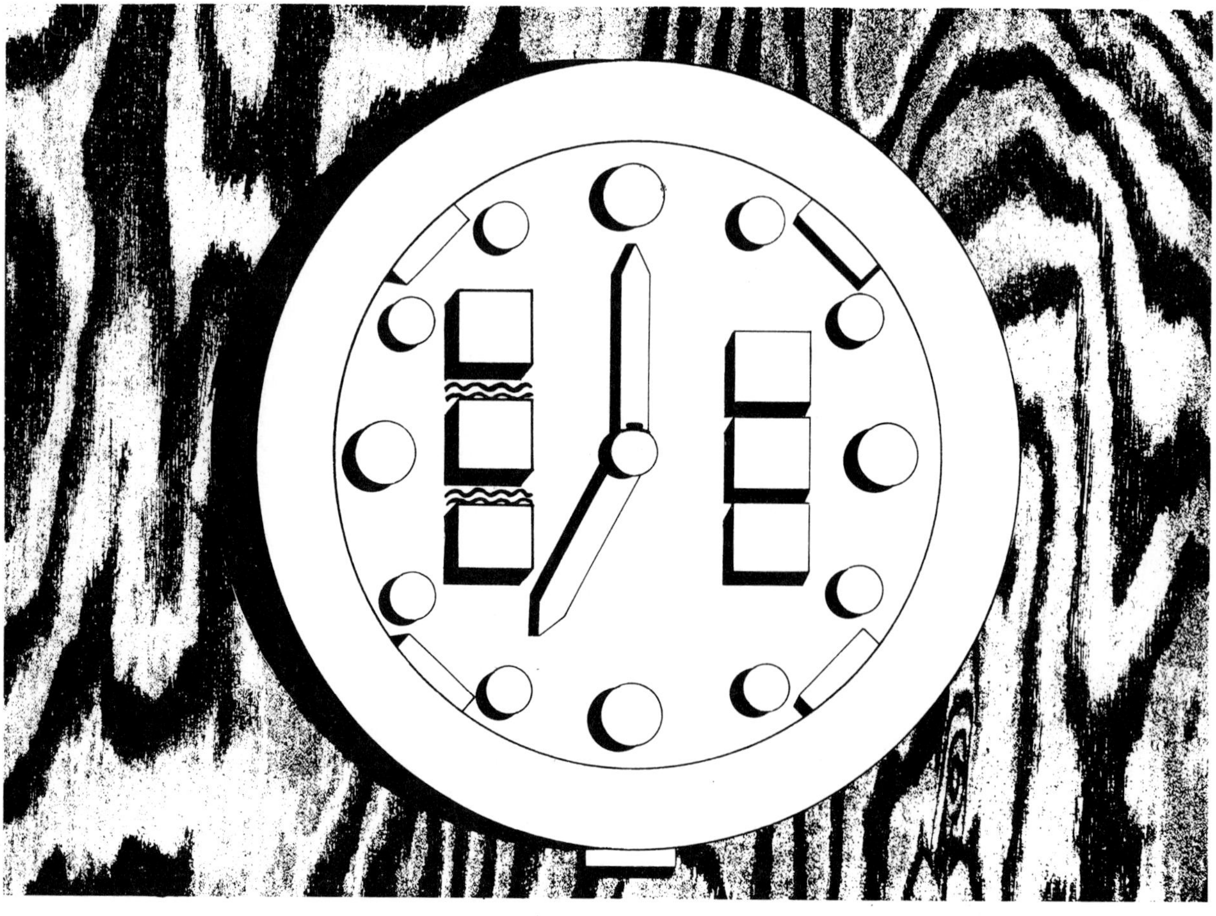

3 Work it out

The professor goes to the village straight away, and takes a lot of photographs. She writes two sentences about each photograph and sends the film to the university. When the film is ready, a woman at the university tries to find the right descriptions for each photograph. Can you match each photograph with its description?

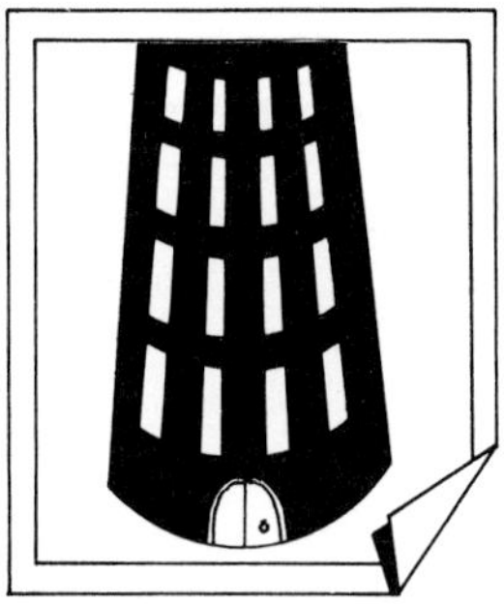
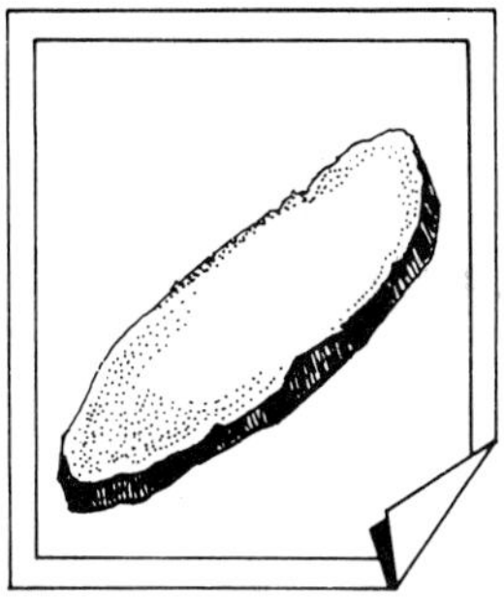
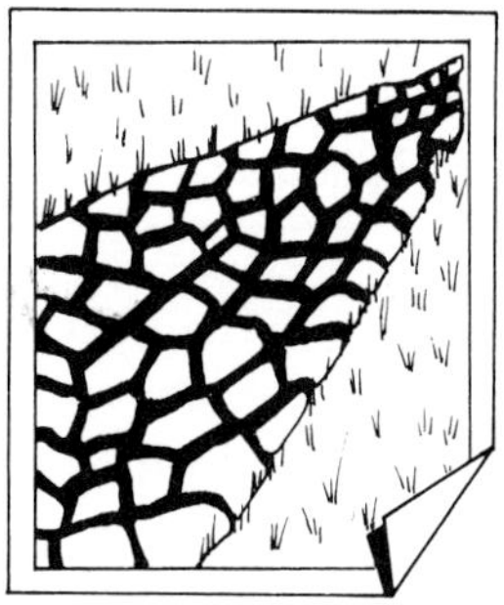
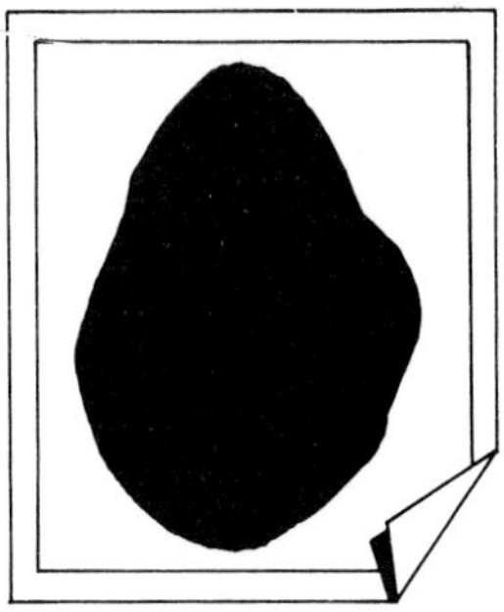

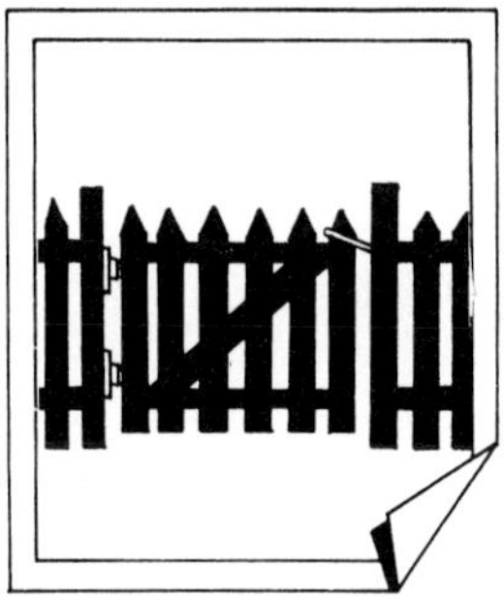

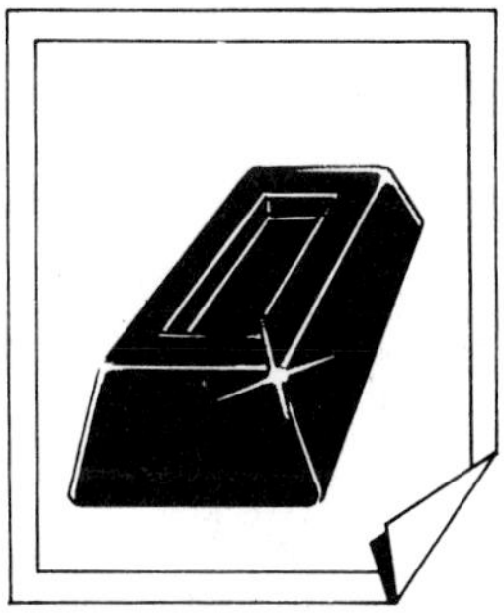

a) There are three. They are over the river.
b) There are hundreds. They are inside the red building.
c) There are two. You can walk between them.
d) There are five. You can walk through four of them.
e) There are three. You can put your arm into them.
f) There is one. It is on top of the three boxes.
g) There are twelve. They are inside the walls.
h) There is a lot. It is between the oil and the wine.
i) There is one. It is in the middle of the village.
j) There are two. They go towards the red building.

4 Hidden village

A journalist sees the photographs and writes a story for his newspaper. The sentences are in the wrong order. Can you sort them out?

Five men leave the camp with the professor at half-past seven in the morning and climb up the mountain. First they measure the ground inside the house. They all go through the big gate. They take the objects to the professor. The professor stays between the walls with a plan of the village. They go to the big stone house at the end of the path. The men go into the village. Sometimes they find plates and other objects. Then they dig with small spades.

5 Fill the gaps

The professor makes a list of all the things she finds. Here is the list for the first day. Where do you think she finds these things?

- three plates
- a water jug
- a shoe
- one hundred and seventy diamonds
- thirty litres of red wine
- ten litres of oil
- twelve fireplaces
- two hundred gold pieces
- twenty kilos of rice
- a cooking pot
- fourteen stone beds

6 Talk to the press

The professor talks to the journalist on the radio. You are the professor. Can you answer the questions?

Journalist: Are there many tall buildings?
Professor:
Journalist: Are there many gates?
Professor:
Journalist: Are there many stone boxes?
Professor:
Journalist: Is there much rice?
Professor:

Journalist: Is there much wine?
Professor:
Journalist: Are there many beds?
Professor:
Journalist: Are there many cooking pots?
Professor:
Journalist: Are there many houses?
Professor:
Journalist: Is there much oil?
Professor:

7 Find the message

One day the professor sends a message to the university. She doesn't talk on the radio telephone, she uses Morse Code. Morse is a real code. Many people use it all over the world to send messages by lamp or radio. Each letter is made of dots (.) and dashes (–).

A	.–	F	..–.	K	–.–	P	.––.	U	..–
B	–...	G	––.	L	.–..	Q	––.–	V	...–
C	–.–.	H	....	M	––	R	.–.	W	.––
D	–..	I	..	N	–.	S	...	X	–..–
E	.	J	.–––	O	–––	T	–	Y	–.––
								Z	––..

The professor sends this message. Use the code to work out what she says.

– / .... / . / .–. / . // .– / .–. / . // .–. / ––– / –... / –... / . / .–. / ... //
––– / –. // – / .... / . // .. / ... / .–.. / .– / –. / –.. // .–– / . // .– /
.–. / . // –.–. / ––– / –– / .. / –. / ––. // .... / ––– / –– / . // .–– /
.. / – / .... // – / .... / . // ––. / ––– / .–.. / –.. //

UNIT EIGHT
She can sleep in the garden

1 Listen

Robert is a farmer. He lives on his farm in the country, but every Tuesday afternoon he comes to town. He sleeps at his mother's house and then goes on to market on Wednesday.

Robert's mother wants him to find a wife, but Robert doesn't want to get married. He has his farm and his animals and is quite happy.

But one day Robert telephones his mother. Listen to their conversation.

2 Listen and write

Robert gets this form from the market. Can you help him to fill it in?

Animal for sale

Type of animal ______________________

Colour of fur ______________________

Colour of eyes ______________________

Is the animal large or small? ______________________

What does the animal eat? ______________________

What does the animal drink? ______________________

Has the animal got a cage? ______________________

3 Misunderstanding

Sally Mitchell lives by the river, near to Robert's farm. In their telephone conversation, Robert's mother thinks he is talking about Sally. But if Robert is talking about Sally, he says some surprising things! Listen to the conversation again. How many surprising things can you find?

4 Who says what?

Robert is still talking about Nancy. His mother is still talking about Sally. These are some of the things they say. Who says what?

a) I'm going to take her to the market.
b) I'm going to take her to the cinema.
c) She's got a hairy face.
d) Have you got any dry grass?
e) Can she play the piano?
f) Can she sleep in the garage?
g) Give her a bucket of water.
h) Give her a bottle of wine.
i) Are you going to marry her?
j) She doesn't bite.
k) I'm going to sell her.
l) She's got white fur.
m) She wears a white fur coat.
n) She's got a beautiful smile.

5 What does she say?

Robert's mother is very surprised. She telephones Sally and asks some questions. Sally is also very surprised, but she answers politely. What does she say?

Robert's mother:	Are you Miss Mitchell?
Sally:	
Robert's mother:	Do you live by the river?
Sally:	
Robert's mother:	How often do you eat roses?
Sally:	
Robert's mother:	Do you eat grass?
Sally:	
Robert's mother:	Why do you sleep in the garden?
Sally:	
Robert's mother:	Can you sleep in a box?
Sally:	
Robert's mother:	Where do you sleep, Nancy?
Sally:	I'm called Sally. Nancy is a goat.
Robert's mother:	Oh, I see! Now I understand!

6 True or false?

When Robert arrives with the goat, his mother tells him about Sally. Robert laughs. He knows Sally, but not very well. He talks about Sally, but he makes some mistakes. Are these sentences true or false?

a) Her name is Sally Williams.
b) She's got a pretty face.
c) Her hair is short.
d) She hasn't got a fur coat.
e) She's got blue eyes.
f) She lives by the river.
g) She's small.
h) She hasn't got a telephone.

7 Work it out

Robert goes to the market on Wednesday and looks at the board beside the gate. Usually there is a list of animals on the board, but today it is very windy. All the letters are on the ground. Can you help Robert to find the names of the seven animals for sale?

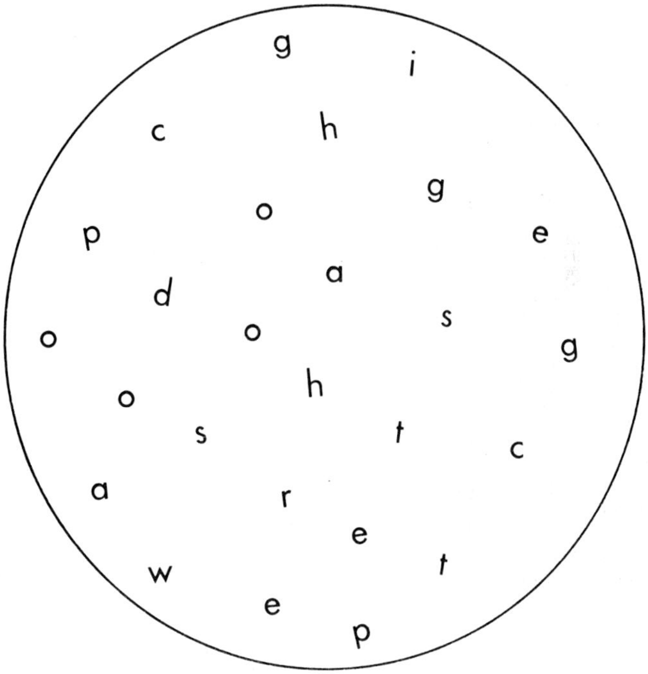

UNIT NINE
The party

1 Listen

Jane and Lucy are having a party tonight at their flat. This morning they made a list of food, drink and other things they need.

cheese
sausages
tomatoes
lettuce
cucumber
bread
butter
eggs
cake
biscuits
small cakes
peanuts
potato crisps
chocolate mints

red wine
white wine
beer
lemonade
Coke
coffee
cream
sugar

At five o'clock Lucy telephones Jane. She asks about the list. Look at the list and listen to their conversation.

2 Listen and write

a) What is Lucy going to buy?
b) What is she going to borrow?
c) What do they still need?

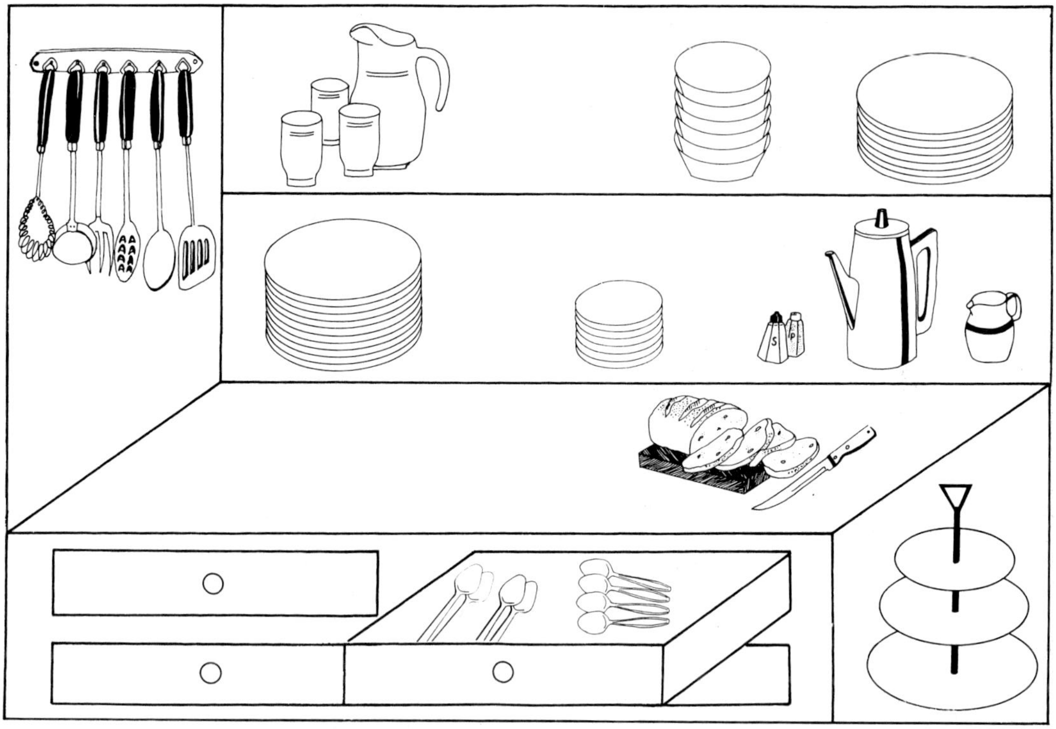

3 Check the details

Look at the picture of the girls' kitchen, and then look at the menu below.

a) What do they need to serve supper?
b) Have they got all the things they need?
c) What haven't they got?

MENU

peanuts and crisps
wine and cheese
egg and sausage salad
bread and butter
biscuits and cakes
coffee with cream, sugar and mints

To drink: red and white wine
beer
lemonade
coke

4 Fill the gaps

At the party Lucy danced with Bruce. The music was very loud and she couldn't hear every word. This is what Lucy heard. What did Bruce say?

'This _____ very nice party. _____ glad I came. I like this music _____ much, but it's a bit too _____. _____ hear what you _____ saying. Do you _____ dancing? So do _____. Would you _____ to come _____ a dance on Saturday night? Good. I'll come at eight _____ clock, and we'll go _____ my car.'

5 Talk to Lucy

It was a very good party. Everyone danced and ate and talked a lot. Lucy and Jane went to bed very late. In the morning they started to clean the flat, but most things were not in the right place.

Lucy asked, 'Where's the cheese?'	Jane said, 'We ate it.'
Lucy asked, 'Where's the lemonade?'	Jane said, 'It's in the fridge.'

Lucy asked these questions, too. What did Jane say?

a) Where are the sausages?
b) Where are the cans of beer?
c) Where's the red wine?
d) Where are my brother's plates?
e) Where are our wine glasses?
f) Where's the lettuce?
g) Where are my car keys?
h) Where's Mary's cake?
i) Where are the chairs?

6 Work it out

Lucy wrote the instructions for serving some food and drink. Now they are mixed up. Which information is for which food?

– eggs	serve them straight from the packet
– sausages	serve with cream and sugar
– red wine	cook for ten minutes
– coffee	serve at twenty degrees centigrade
– lettuce	cook in boiling water for six minutes
– small cakes	wash and serve
– peanuts	put a little icing on the top of each one

7 Find the letter

Here is a game which they played at the party.
Can you find the letter which is missing in each group of words below?

–akes	–arty	–read
–oke	–iece of –a–er	–utter
–heese	–eanuts	–iscuits
–ans of beer	–lates	–ruce
–offee	–eo–le	
–hairs		

UNIT TEN
It isn't lost, Mr Evans!

1 Listen

Stephen works for an accountancy firm called Evans and Sons. Three hours ago Mr Evans asked Stephen to go to a shop in the town to collect a briefcase. There were important papers in the briefcase. But Stephen didn't come back.

At last he telephones. Mr Evans is very angry. Listen to their conversation.

2 Listen and write

Mr Evans telephones the police. He explains what happened to the briefcase. Here are the questions the policeman asked. What did Mr Evans say?

Policeman: What's in the briefcase?
Mr Evans:
Policeman: Who collected it from the shop?
Mr Evans:
Policeman: Where did he go?
Mr Evans:
Policeman: Why?
Mr Evans:
Policeman: Why did he take the briefcase?
Mr Evans:
Policeman: Who picked it up?
Mr Evans:
Policeman: Where did she go?
Mr Evans:
Policeman: Why?
Mr Evans:
Policeman: Why didn't her boss look at it carefully?
Mr Evans:
Policeman: Where did he take it?
Mr Evans:
Policeman: Where is it now?
Mr Evans:

3 Who said what?

The policeman also talked to Stephen, the woman, and her boss in Rio de Janeiro. Here are their answers. Who said what?

a) I knew it wasn't my briefcase. My briefcase has my name and address on the handle.
b) I stayed at the garage and telephoned the woman.
c) I was on my way to the airport, so I didn't look at it carefully.
d) She picked it up and left. I didn't notice until it was too late.
e) I drove to London immediately.
f) My own briefcase was with my other luggage at the airport.
g) I've still got her briefcase.
h) I haven't got a briefcase at all.
i) I've got two briefcases.
j) I'm going to send the briefcase back on the next plane.

4 Sort it out

Stephen makes some notes, but he gets mixed up. Can you help?

The boss is	made of black leather, with a name on the handle.
The woman's briefcase is	flying through the air at the moment.
Mr Evans is	in a briefcase.
The plane is	very sorry.
The important papers are	a secretary.
I am	very angry.
The woman is	going to work in Rio de Janeiro.

5 Fill the gaps

Stephen takes the briefcase to the address on the handle. A beautiful woman answers the door. Stephen asks her, 'Are you Janet Richards?' She says, 'Yes, I am.'

Here is what Stephen says. What does Janet reply?

Stephen: How do you do?
Janet:
Stephen: Is this your briefcase?
Janet:
Stephen: You left it at the petrol station.
Janet:
Stephen: Did you drive all the way to London yesterday?
Janet:
Stephen: Aren't you tired?
Janet:

Stephen: You haven't got our briefcase, have you?
Janet:
Stephen: You gave it to your boss?
Janet:
Stephen: And he's in Rio de Janeiro?
Janet:
Stephen: But he's going to send it back?
Janet:
Stephen: Would you like to have dinner with me?
Janet:
Stephen: What time shall I pick you up?
Janet:

6 Find the right words

The dinner wasn't good. Stephen writes a note on the bill.

'This restaurant is awful. The soup was awful, the meat was awful, the potatoes were awful, the gateau was awful, the coffee was awful, the wine was awful, the waiters were awful, and the music was awful.'

Janet says, 'You can't give them that note. You can't say *awful* all the time. Use different words.'

Stephen begins: 'This restaurant is awful. The soup was cold . . .'

Can you help him finish the note?

7 Find the message

Three months later Mr Evans comes to work and finds small pieces of paper in his ashtray. Stephen wrote a note and then tore it up. There is a word on each piece of paper. Mr Evans puts the words in order, and then smiles. What did Stephen's note say? Start with 'I am . . .'

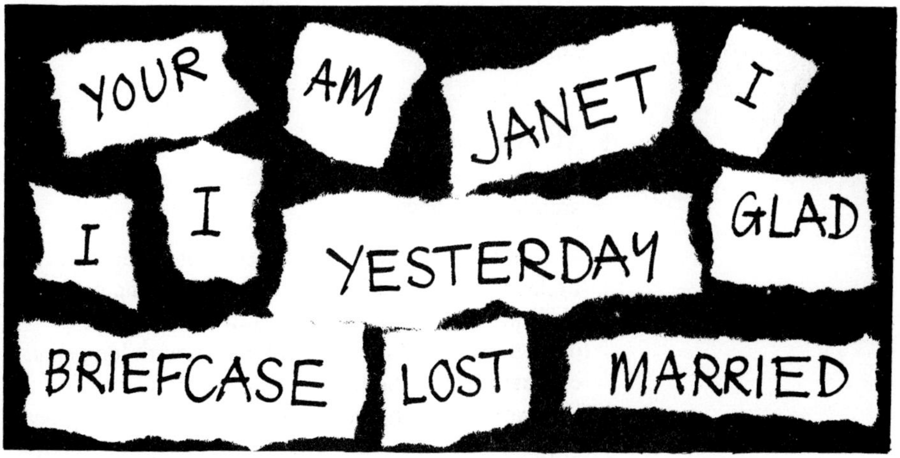

UNIT ELEVEN

Consolidation: It was long and thin with big teeth

1 Listen

You work in a zoo, where you drive a lorry and look after the animals. One morning the zoo manager telephones you. He's very worried. Someone got into the zoo during the night and broke open a lot of cages. Some animals escaped and now they're in the park, next to the zoo.

You take your lorry and some cages, and drive to the main gates of the park. The manager talks to you on the radio in your lorry, and you drive exactly where he tells you.

Start at the main gates at the top of the plan. Remember that the ticket office is on your left as you drive in.

2 Listen and write

Write a list of the animals you find on your way through the park.

3 Try again

Which animals didn't you find? Take the lorry back and try to find them. Start at the back gate.

4 Work it out

People tell you about the animals in the park. Here is what they say. Which animals did they see?

a) I saw something big and grey with a long nose.
b) I saw something tall and thin with a long neck.
c) I saw something long and thin with big teeth.
d) I saw something small and brown with long ears.
e) I saw something long and thin with no legs.
f) I saw something brown and hairy with a long beard.
g) I saw something brown and hairy with big teeth.

ROSE GARDEN
TICKET OFFICE
BRIDGE
SHOP
SHOP
MAIN ROAD
SWINGS
CAFE
GRASS
BACK GATE
CHILDREN'S MAZE
FLOWER GARDEN
ZOO BACK GATE

5 Talk to the visitors

When the park is open again, people ask you questions. Can you help them?

a) Where can I look at the roses?
b) Where can we have a picnic?
c) Where can I buy an ice-cream?
d) Where can I sail a boat?
e) Where can the children play?
f) Where can I sit down?
g) Where can I find a seat?
h) Where can I play tennis?
i) Where can I buy a ticket?
j) Where are the goldfish?
k) Where can I see the animals?

6 Give directions

Someone stops you outside the tennis court. He asks how to get out of the park. Can you help him?

7 Word game

Can you find the names of things which were in the park? You can read up or down, backwards or forwards.

Q	S	E	E	R	T	E	D	S	T
N	W	A	G	A	T	E	S	R	O
D	I	L	D	A	Y	T	T	E	S
N	N	O	I	L	E	L	A	W	N
O	G	I	R	A	F	F	E	O	A
P	O	B	B	K	G	A	S	L	K
G	A	E	E	E	A	C	A	F	E
M	T	A	O	B	Q	S	H	O	P